Tarot Meditations

A Journal for Self Discovery

Tarot Meditations

A Journal for Self Discovery

By

Expanding Dimensions

Illustrated by

Christopher Wilkey

R. C. Linnell Publishing

TAROT MEDITATIONS: A JOURNAL FOR SELF DISCOVERY

Cover design by Dave Davis

Illustrated by Christopher Wilkey

Photos by Joy Vest

ISBN 10: 098-40025-8-8

ISBN 13: 978-0-9840025-8-0

Published by:

R.C. Linnell Publishing

Louisville, KY 40205

www.LinnellPublishing.com

Other publications by Expanding Dimensions:
Today's Journey Tarot (card deck) ISBN: 978-0-7643-3905-9
Today's Journey Tarot: A Traveler's Guide ISBN: 978-0-9840025-6-6
www.TodaysJourneyTarot.com

Other publication by Expanding Dimension members:
Lessons: The Wisdom Within Each Moment by Sue McAdams
ISBN: 978-0-9840025-3-5
Journeys: A Guide to Group Meditation by Ben Perry
ASIN: B001DV3PI4
www.benperrymeditations.com

This book is dedicated to the
enlightenment and wisdom within each of us
and to the
supporters of *Today's Journey Tarot*
for their encouragement, commitment, and inspiration.

CONTENTS

CONTENTS (CONT.)

INTRODUCTION

The Tarot has traditionally been used as a tool for divination, but it is much more. As a powerful instrument for self-discovery, it teaches us that the answers to all of our questions are within. The deck of seventy eight cards opens the door to the subconscious mind and allows it to be understood. Its value is essential and universal. Heritage, social background, economic status, age, race, or gender does not matter. The cards contain layer upon layer of knowledge that directly relate to every aspect of human behavior, from the most basic mundane questions to the highest levels of spiritual truth. The language the Tarot speaks is collective symbology. Colors, numbers, images, and metaphors convey its wisdom.

Understanding the cards is similar to interpreting the images from dreams. Dream symbols are the subconscious mind's way of communicating with us. The cards' images work the same way. When we contemplate their symbols, the subconscious mind becomes engaged and has a conversation with the Tarot, even though we are not consciously aware of it.

The Tarot also teaches that through the subconscious mind we discover our connection to the Universe and everything within it. When we meditate we interact with that part of ourselves. The influence of the outside world is diminished as the inner self becomes dominant. Meditation can range from light, relaxed contemplation to a deep altered transcendent state. Through meditation we have the opportunity to become active participants in the conversation between the Tarot and the inner self. We can ask ourselves questions that challenge our traditional beliefs and limitations and discover inner resources of inspiration, empowerment, and growth. The Tarot is one of the most powerful tools available to use in conjunction with meditation, because the intuitive part of the mind responds to its symbolic imagery.

Open new vistas of thought and awareness by meditating with the Tarot. You will get a better understanding of yourself and the cards. The possibilities are endless. For example, you can choose a color, number, symbol, or person from one of the cards and visualize that image in your mind while you meditate. See what associations may come to you, how you feel about the image, or what meaning is revealed. You can also imagine yourself stepping into one of the cards and extending the environment as you look around. Let the cards and your inner self guide you.

How to Use This Journal

The Tarot and meditation are both tools for self-discovery. This journal is designed to provide a progression of steps that gradually opens the mind to each card and its meaning, encouraging a light state of meditation that can even be done while writing. It is not necessary to have experience with meditation or deep states of consciousness to benefit from these exercises. The depictions are from *Today's Journey Tarot* created by Expanding Dimensions and illustrated by Christopher Wilkey, but any traditional Tarot deck can be used. The journey begins with a single word and leads to a Universal Truth the card reveals. The levels can be contemplated in any order, individually or reflected upon as a group. There are no limits.

You can open the journal at random or start at the beginning and work your way through. The card you select is significant to you at this time. Read through the information first and determine what level or levels you will be focusing on. Below are some suggestions for working with each step. Do not limit yourself to these ideas or feel that you have to answer every question, they are only designed to begin your internal dialogue.

Sit or lie down in a comfortable position and take a few deep breaths in and out slowly. Allow yourself to relax. Focus only on this moment and your breathing. If your mind wanders gently bring it back to your breath. You should be in a calm, peaceful, light meditative state. Continue to relax and begin to think about what you have just read and let your mind flow freely as you consider these thoughts. Allow yourself time to fully explore the information. You can either write about your experiences when you are finished or journal as you go. The journal is a record of your thoughts and insights as you contemplate each card.

Contemplate: This is a key word associated with the card's meaning. When you repeat the word in your mind, what is the first thing that comes to you? How does this word relate to you and your life? What is this word telling you about yourself? Do any specific images or scenarios come to mind? Does this word lead to other words? What do they mean to you?

Ask Yourself: This is the central question the card is asking you. How does this question make you feel? Do you resist its implications? Is it challenging you to be completely honest with yourself? Does this step require some action on your part? Does it lead to other questions?

Tell Yourself: This is an empowering personal statement. It is meant to be used as an affirmation or a mantra to help you understand more about the card and yourself. It may even assist in answering the previous question. If you internalize this statement, what changes would it make in your life? Can you see yourself making those changes?

Know: This is a Universal Truth the card teaches. What is your first impression of this statement? Do you agree with it? Can you embrace it? How does it relate to you at this time? How does knowing this change you? What other truths does this card suggest to you?

An example meditation using this process follows Key 0, Beginning.

This journal includes space for you to write your experiences: how you feel, what comes to mind, what you are inspired to do, and new levels of understanding the Tarot has opened for you. You can return again and again to the same card and still learn more. The next time you select the card, you can incorporate the notes you have taken into the new meditation for another level of self-discovery, and add new insights to your journal entry. Images from dreams and personal experiences relating to your meditations can also be noted.

Expanded meditations interacting with the images from *Today's Journey Tarot* are provided throughout this journal. These "Experiences" are examples of other ways to interact with the Tarot while meditating, which can be done with any card from any deck.

KEY 0 BEGINNING
(THE FOOL)

Every moment has the potential for a new beginning: a thought, idea, or action which leads to self-discovery.

CONTEMPLATE: Faith

ASK YOURSELF: Am I open to new experiences and discoveries?

TELL YOURSELF: I do not fear the unknown.

KNOW: Faith is needed to trust inner guidance.

Notes:

KEY 0 BEGINNING EXAMPLE MEDITATION

Choose a comfortable place where you can relax. Hold your journal if you wish to write as you meditate. If you do not want to journal while you relax, keep it nearby for quick access. When you are ready close your eyes and take a few deep breaths in and out slowly. Let go of what you were doing before this moment. Let go of what you may need to do next. Just relax and focus on your breathing. Slowly count backwards from number ten to number one. Allow yourself to relax more and more with each count. From this comfortable state of awareness you are ready to begin an internal conversation. Allow the information to flow into your mind. Do not try to force or restrict it. Consider this statement, "Every moment has the potential for a new beginning: a thought, idea, or action which leads to self-discovery." Contemplate the word "faith". When you repeat it in your mind, what is the first thing that comes to you? How does it relate to you and your life right now? What thoughts or images come to mind? After you spend a few minutes with the word faith, ask yourself "am I open to new experiences and discoveries?" Be honest with yourself. How does this question make you feel? Do you resist it? Does it challenge you to do something? Does it lead to other questions? After you have contemplated this question tell yourself, "I do not fear the unknown." Repeat this affirmation a few times in your mind. If you internalize this statement, how would it change your life? Spend a few moments visualizing yourself making those changes. Know "faith is needed to trust inner guidance." Spend a few more minutes understanding what Key 0 is trying to teach you. What other truths does this card suggest to you? When you are ready, take a few more deep breaths. Count forward from one to ten and open your eyes.

Notes:

KEY 1 MANIFESTATION (THE MAGICIAN)

There are no limits to creative power. Every thought, word, and deed shapes reality.

CONTEMPLATE: Creation

ASK YOURSELF: What are the actions I'm taking today building for tomorrow?

TELL YOURSELF: I am aware of what I am manifesting.

KNOW: Active participation is needed to responsibly create.

Notes:

KEY 2 WISDOM
(THE HIGH PRIESTESS)

The subconscious mind contains all the answers we seek. This inner truth appears hidden, but is always available.

CONTEMPLATE: Truth

ASK YOURSELF: Am I asking myself the right questions?

TELL YOURSELF: I trust the wisdom within me.

KNOW: The knowledge revealed within is your truth.

Notes:

Key 3 Creativity
(The Empress)

Creativity is not limited to artistic pursuits. The birth of a new idea can impact every facet of life.

Contemplate: Fertility

Ask Yourself: Am I using my imagination effectively?

Tell Yourself: Whatever I can imagine, I can do.

Know: A fertile mind yields an unending harvest.

Notes:

Key 4 Law
(The Emperor)

The Universe is in Divine order. Acceptance of this is the beginning of freedom, struggling against it is ineffective and changes nothing.

Contemplate: Acceptance

Ask Yourself: What am I resisting that I cannot change?

Tell Yourself: I trust that everything is as it should be.

Know: The only thing you can change is yourself.

Notes:

KEY 5 TRADITION
(THE HIEROPHANT)

The past is a foundation that should be remembered, but rigidly following tradition limits growth.

CONTEMPLATE: Limitation

ASK YOURSELF: Do I think for myself or blindly follow the beliefs of others?

TELL YOURSELF: I am not afraid to be myself.

KNOW: It is possible to be part of society and maintain individuality.

Notes:

Key 6 Union
(The Lovers)

There must be a balance of body, mind, and spirit to develop awareness of the Divine within.

Contemplate: Spirituality

Ask Yourself: Where do I find spiritual truth?

Tell Yourself: I am Divine.

Know: Remembering the connection between everything in the Universe is bliss.

Notes:

Key 7 Control
(The Chariot)

Mental self-control eliminates doubt and leads to infinite possibilities.

Contemplate: Freedom

Ask Yourself: Are doubts holding me back?

Tell Yourself: I control my thoughts.

Know: A mind free of doubt can accomplish anything.

Notes:

KEY 8 FORTITUDE
(STRENGTH)

Spiritual strength is more powerful than any physical force. It is always present, never diminishes, and resides within everyone.

CONTEMPLATE: Power

ASK YOURSELF: Where do I draw strength from?

TELL YOURSELF: I am empowered.

KNOW: The spiritual strength within overcomes disbelief.

Notes:

KEY 9 GUIDANCE
(THE HERMIT)

Sometimes it is necessary to seek knowledge. It is not a sign of weakness to ask for help, we are meant to learn from one another.

CONTEMPLATE: Knowledge

ASK YOURSELF: Am I open to the guidance being offered to me?

TELL YOURSELF: I am not alone.

KNOW: The Universe offers infinite resources of wisdom.

Notes:

The Key 9 Experience

Consider a few questions you might have on your mind at this time. They can concern any area of your life; personal, professional, or spiritual. Begin your relaxation process and when you are comfortable, close your eyes. Imagine you are standing in the center of large modern library. Polished wood floors lead to row after row of books. The arched ceiling contains skylights that allow sunlight to brighten the room. You feel yourself drawn to a carpeted area where wooden tables and chairs have been arranged to read, study, or work. One of these tables has several books on it already opened to specific pages. On these pages you will find the answers to your questions. You may even find answers to questions you didn't even know you had. Spend some time at this table. Study the books. You may find pictures, symbols, or personal messages on these pages. When you are ready, open your eyes and journal your experiences. You can return to the library again and again to find the answers you seek.

Notes:

KEY 10 LIFE
(THE WHEEL OF FORTUNE)

Life is filled with highs and lows. How we perceive what happens to us determines the quality of our journey.

CONTEMPLATE: Perception

ASK YOURSELF: What do I need to see differently?

TELL YOURSELF: I know everything is alright.

KNOW: Changing perspective changes everything.

Notes:

KEY 11 KARMA
(JUSTICE)

The law of cause and effect is just. Everything equals out eventually, even if it is different than what is expected.

CONTEMPLATE: Justice

ASK YOURSELF: Am I trying to control how things should be?

TELL YOURSELF: I release expectations and remain positive.

KNOW: Karma does not punish, it restores balance without discrimination.

Notes:

KEY 12 CHOICE
(THE HANGED MAN)

Sometimes we prefer comfortable stagnation instead of risking the unknown by making a choice.

CONTEMPLATE: Choice

ASK YOURSELF: What decision do I not want to make?

TELL YOURSELF: I accept that there are no wrong choices.

KNOW: The decision not to choose is still a choice.

Notes:

Key 13 Transition
(Death)

Change is an exercise in growth and has the potential for transformation. Resistance to it is wasted energy.

Contemplate: Change

Ask Yourself: Do I fear the unknown?

Tell Yourself: I am ready for whatever happens.

Know: Without change, growth is not possible.

Notes:

KEY 14 DISCERNMENT
(TEMPERANCE)

When one aspect of our life is out of harmony it affects every other area. Strive for choices that create balance.

CONTEMPLATE: Balance

ASK YOURSELF: What areas of my life are out of balance?

TELL YOURSELF: I release the need for stress.

KNOW: Sound judgment leads to a harmonious life.

Notes:

Key 15 Materialism
(The Devil)

Fulfillment derived only from physical gratification is a limiting and destructive illusion. The material world is to be enjoyed, not worshipped.

Contemplate: Illusion

Ask Yourself: Do I place too much value on material attainment?

Tell Yourself: I release attachments.

Know: Illusions do not endure.

Notes:

KEY 16 INTERVENTION
(THE TOWER)

Disruption is a natural part of life. We can choose to fight against it or seek solutions and move forward.

CONTEMPLATE: Opportunity

ASK YOURSELF: What am I learning from my experiences?

TELL YOURSELF: I see challenges as opportunities.

KNOW: Order can be found, even within chaos.

Notes:

Key 17 Meditation
(The Star)

Meditation is a powerful instrument for self-discovery, insight, and inspiration. A quiet mind hears the answers to all of life's mysteries.

Contemplate: Inspiration

Ask Yourself: Where do I find peace?

Tell Yourself: I open myself to the Universe.

Know: Yourself.

Notes:

KEY 18 INTUITION
(THE MOON)

The subconscious mind communicates through intuition. We all have the ability to perceive this endless resource of information and guidance.

CONTEMPLATE: Perception

ASK YOURSELF: Do I trust what I feel or do I validate my feelings through others?

TELL YOURSELF: I do what I believe is right.

KNOW: Feelings are the expression of inner truth.

Notes:

The Key 18 Experience

Begin your relaxation process and when you are ready, close your eyes. With your mind's eye, see yourself seated at a small wooden table covered with an indigo colored cloth. The only light in the room comes from a large crystal ball in the center of the table. Its surface is smooth and clear, mesmerizing to look upon. You wait for the reader to arrive, anticipating what she might say. Soon, she sits down across from you. With a warm smile she fills the room with positive energy. Nothing negative can enter. You feel instantly at ease with this person. She begins to speak. Be open to what she tells you. It is significant to you at this time. Spend a few moments here with the reader. Ask questions and find answers. She will indicate when the reading is over. At that time open your eyes and begin to journal your experiences. The crystal ball reader will be there whenever you are ready for another reading.

Notes:

Key 19 Illumination
(The Sun)

When we live fully in the present moment, our spirit is liberated and we experience true joy.

Contemplate: Liberation

Ask Yourself: What restrains me?

Tell Yourself: I release limitations and choose freedom.

Know: Illumination exposes hidden restrictions.

Notes:

KEY 20 AWARENESS
(JUDGEMENT)

Be mindful of opportunities. They often come from unexpected sources.

CONTEMPLATE: Mindfulness

ASK YOURSELF: Am I seeing all the possibilities?

TELL YOURSELF: I am aware.

KNOW: With mindfulness all questions are answered.

Notes:

KEY 21 COMPLETION
(THE WORLD)

Every ending is a new beginning. What has been learned should be integrated into our lives and shared with others.

CONTEMPLATE: Achievement

ASK YOURSELF: Do I celebrate my accomplishments?

TELL YOURSELF: I am ready for new challenges.

KNOW: The purpose of personal success is its contribution to the world.

Notes:

One of Fire
(Ace of Wands)

There is an unlimited supply of energy in the Universe. If we can learn to utilize this force it has the power to sustain us.

Contemplate: Power

Ask Yourself: Where does my power reside?

Tell Yourself: I begin to direct my energy effectively.

Know: The power of the Universe exists within everything.

Notes:

Two of Fire
(Two of Wands)

Optimism is an ingredient of success. We can only turn our passions into realities if we believe we can.

Contemplate: Hope

Ask Yourself: Do my doubts affect my success?

Tell Yourself: I believe in myself.

Know: Hope has the power to overcome doubt.

Notes:

Three of Fire
(Three of Wands)

When we are working in harmony with the Universe, our passion will be fulfilled. Unseen influences support your goals.

Contemplate: Success

Ask Yourself: Do I nurture my accomplishments?

Tell Yourself: I work hard to achieve success.

Know: Commitment determines outcome.

Notes:

The Three of Fire Experience

Begin your relaxation process and when you are comfortable, close your eyes. Imagine you are standing outside the entrance to a lighting store. Through large plate glass windows you can see lamps, chandeliers, track lights, and various other forms of lighting. They are all warmly glowing and inviting. See yourself opening the door and going into the shop. As you walk through the store you can feel the energy of this place. There is a feeling of excitement and hopefulness. You can also sense confidence and success. While you browse, these energies begin to move into your body. Spend some time looking around and gathering these energies into you. When you are ready, open your eyes and begin journaling your experiences. You can return to the shop anytime your energies are low or you need a confidence boost.

Notes:

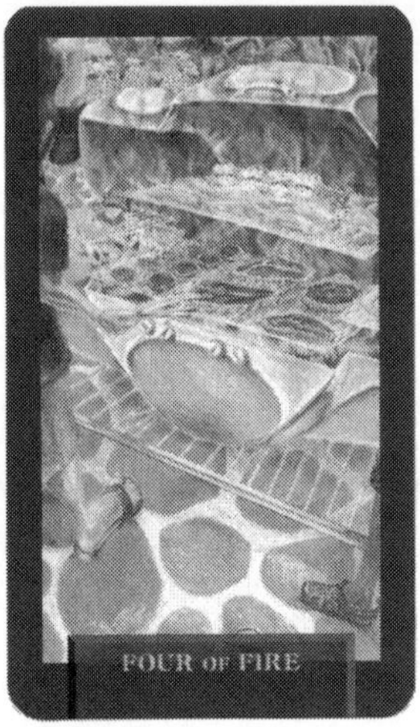

FOUR OF FIRE
(FOUR OF WANDS)

It is important to recognize the abundance in our lives. An attitude of celebration is essential to attract prosperity.

CONTEMPLATE: Prosperity

ASK YOURSELF: Do I appreciate my abundance in all its forms?

TELL YOURSELF: I am thankful for what I have.

KNOW: Life is meant to be celebrated and enjoyed.

Notes:

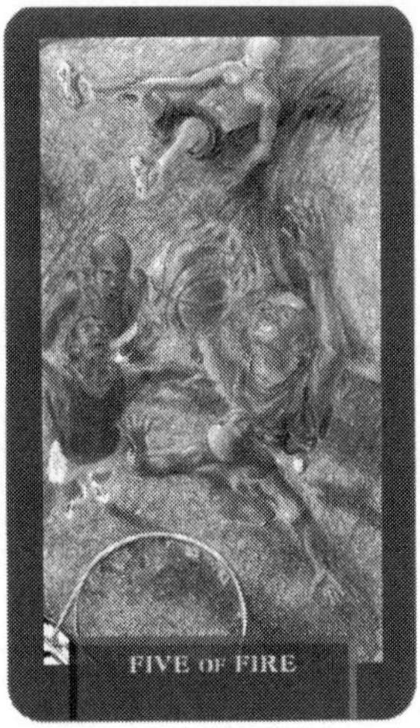

Five of Fire
(Five of Wands)

We perceive that life is full of turmoil. It requires focus to rise above or remove ourselves from the confusion.

Contemplate: Focus

Ask Yourself: Where is my life out of control?

Tell Yourself: Inner peace is my reality.

Know: Chaos is an illusion.

Notes:

SIX OF FIRE
(SIX OF WANDS)

Becoming accomplished in any area makes us leaders. We serve as examples for others.

CONTEMPLATE: Leadership

ASK YOURSELF: What are my accomplishments?

TELL YOURSELF: I am a leader and what I do affects others.

KNOW: Victory should be shared, contributing to the success of the whole.

Notes:

SEVEN OF FIRE
(SEVEN OF WANDS)

We always get what we ask for, along with the consequences. Adversity comes with any situation and can be a catalyst for failure if we do not persevere.

CONTEMPLATE: Perseverance

ASK YOURSELF: Am I doing what I want to do in spite of the demands?

TELL YOURSELF: I accept life's challenges.

KNOW: Every experience has benefits and times of adversity.

Notes:

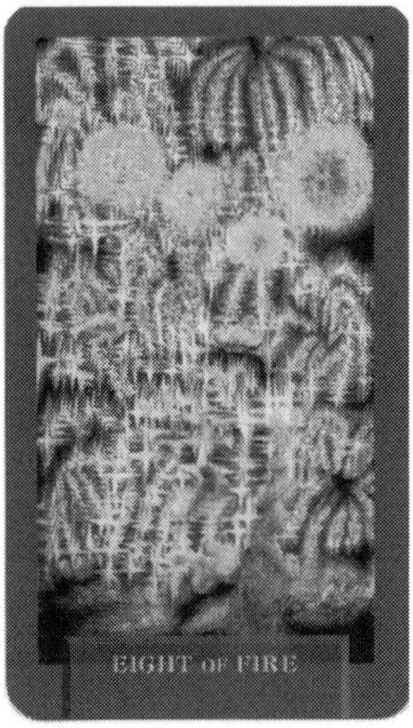

EIGHT OF FIRE
(EIGHT OF WANDS)

Uncontrolled energy is a force that can be intense, confusing, and fleeting. It must understood, then harnessed to be productive.

CONTEMPLATE: Energy

ASK YOURSELF: Where do I focus my energy?

TELL YOURSELF: I am in control.

KNOW: Energy must be used wisely.

Notes:

NINE OF FIRE
(NINE OF WANDS)

There is a fine line between safety and fear. Isolation does not keep us secure.

CONTEMPLATE: Security

ASK YOURSELF: Do my fears limit me?

TELL YOURSELF: I am safe.

KNOW: When you give up freedom for security you will have neither.

Notes:

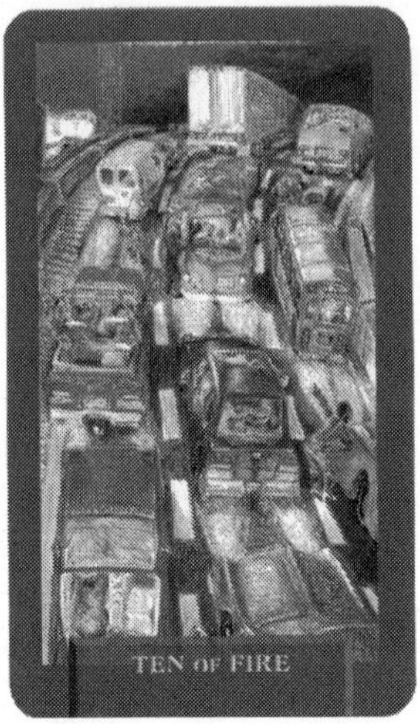

TEN OF FIRE
(TEN OF WANDS)

It is normal to experience moments of frustration. Becoming angry about things that are out of our control is unproductive.

CONTEMPLATE: Control

ASK YOURSELF: Do my frustrations lead to anger?

TELL YOURSELF: I am responsible for my reactions.
KNOW: Everything passes eventually.

Notes:

CHILD OF FIRE
(PAGE OF WANDS)

We should cultivate our passions, but focusing on one thing and excluding everything else is an obsession.

CONTEMPLATE: Obsession

ASK YOURSELF: Are there areas of my life I neglect?

TELL YOURSELF: I use my energy productively.

KNOW: Directed and developed passion can accomplish anything.

Notes:

YOUTH OF FIRE
(KNIGHT OF WANDS)

We are all driven by impulses. The goal should be to strive for balance between safety and recklessness.

CONTEMPLATE: Impulse

ASK YOURSELF: Am I afraid to take risks?

TELL YOURSELF: It is okay to take a chance.

KNOW: Without risk takers, there would be no progress.

Notes:

Mother of Fire
(Queen of Wands)

When we are strong, confident and work hard to fulfill our goals we are successful.

Contemplate: Confidence

Ask Yourself: Do I believe in myself?

Tell Yourself: I create my own success.

Know: With confidence and commitment no goal is out of reach.

Notes:

The Mother of Fire Experience

Begin your relaxation process and when you are comfortable, close your eyes. See yourself standing outside among a large group of people. The sky is blue and it is a pleasant summer day. In front of you there is a stage with a wooden podium. There is sense of anticipation in the air. You are all waiting for someone to appear. Soon a woman dressed in red crosses the stage, smiling and waving. She is strong, confident, and successful. She approaches the podium and begins to speak. It seems as if the people around you are oblivious to the fact that the woman is speaking directly to you. She brings you a message. Spend some time listening to what the Mother of Fire has to say. When you are ready, open your eyes and begin journaling your experience.

Notes:

FATHER OF FIRE
(KING OF WANDS)

There is great power in focused passion. It creates an attraction that draws to us what we most need to succeed.

CONTEMPLATE: Passion

ASK YOURSELF: Am I doing what is necessary to accomplish my goals?

TELL YOURSELF: I attract my own success.

KNOW: Passion must be directed to be fulfilled.

Notes:

ONE OF WATER
(ACE OF CUPS)

There is an unlimited supply of love in the Universe. This nourishing, pure force is always available to us.

CONTEMPLATE: Love

ASK YOURSELF: Is the love in my life beneficial to me?

TELL YOURSELF: I am lovable.

KNOW: True love is not conditional.

Notes:

Two of Water
(Two of Cups)

In order to be truly committed to anything, personal or professional, we must first love it.

Contemplate: Commitment

Ask Yourself: Do I love without commitment?

Tell Yourself: I am capable of unconditional love.

Know: Commitment allows the realization of full potential.

Notes:

THREE OF WATER
(THREE OF CUPS)

Friendship does not judge. It provides strength, stability, and emotional freedom.

CONTEMPLATE: Friendship

ASK YOURSELF: Am I a good friend?

TELL YOURSELF: I deserve the support I get from those I love.

KNOW: The celebration of life is meant to be shared.

Notes:

Four of Water
(Four of Cups)

Many of us move through life unaware of the constant stream of opportunities available to us.

Contemplate: Opportunity

Ask Yourself: Am I blindly walking through life?

Tell Yourself: I am open to direction from the Universe.

Know: If an opportunity is missed, there will always be another.

Notes:

FIVE OF WATER
(FIVE OF CUPS)

If we are attached to the past, it is impossible to move forward.

CONTEMPLATE: Attachment

ASK YOURSELF: What am I holding on to that needs to be released?

TELL YOURSELF: I live for today.

KNOW: There's a difference between remembrance and attachment.

Notes:

Six of Water
(Six of Cups)

When we play, we should do so without expectations or inhibitions. This form of innocence brings joy to every experience.

Contemplate: Innocence

Ask Yourself: Do I take time to play?

Tell Yourself: Playing is essential to my growth.

Know: The innocence of childhood still exists within.

Notes:

The Six of Water Experience

Begin your relaxation process and when you are comfortable, close your eyes. See yourself outside on a beautiful day. The sky above is blue and you are in a wooded area surrounded by trees. It is peaceful here. A calmness moves over and through you. You follow a small, well-worn dirt path on the ground beneath you. It leads to a creek with gently flowing water. The stones along the side of the creek and under the water are all white. There is a sense of innocence in this place as if it exists for your pleasure alone. Spend some time here at the creek. Be in the moment. Take your shoes off and wade in the water. Enjoy the wonders of this place. Let go of the stresses of being an adult and play. When you are ready, open your eyes and journal your experiences.

Notes:

SEVEN OF WATER
(SEVEN OF CUPS)

Dreams can come true. It is the quality of our belief in them that determines their realization.

CONTEMPLATE: Belief

ASK YOURSELF: Do I really want my dreams to come true?

TELL YOURSELF: I know I can create what I can imagine.

KNOW: All limits are self-imposed.

Notes:

EIGHT OF WATER
(EIGHT OF CUPS)

It is sometimes difficult for us to recognize or accept that everything ends.

CONTEMPLATE: Completion

ASK YOURSELF: What have I finished that I'm not letting go?

TELL YOURSELF: I can move on.

KNOW: Completion is not an ending, it is a new beginning.

Notes:

Nine of Water
(Nine of Cups)

When we live our dreams, we exist in a state of fulfillment. The Universe has responded to our positive, self-assuredness.

Contemplate: Fulfillment

Ask Yourself: Do I have the confidence to fulfill my dreams?

Tell Yourself: I believe in myself.

Know: For every dream there are many opportunities to achieve it.

Notes:

Ten of Water
(Ten of Cups)

Happiness is a choice. It is our responsibility to create it in our relationships and our environment.

Contemplate: Happiness

Ask Yourself: Do I allow myself to be happy?

Tell Yourself: I control my emotions.

Know: Happiness, like all emotions, comes from within.

Notes:

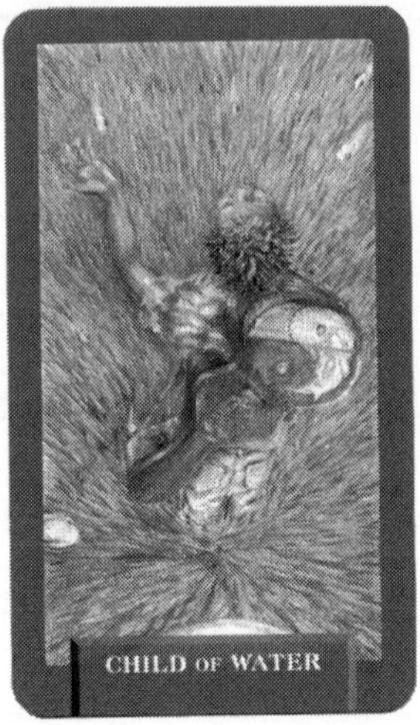

Child of Water
(Page of Cups)

We must continuously be open to the creative energies within and around us. Sensitivity is a spiritual gift that should be encouraged and nurtured.

Contemplate: Sensitivity

Ask Yourself: Do I fear my imagination?

Tell Yourself: I embrace my creativity.

Know: The world would be a drab and boring place without sensitive souls willing to share their imaginations.

Notes:

YOUTH OF WATER
(KNIGHT OF CUPS)

Intense emotions, whether positive or negative, are fleeting. The feeling is real but cannot be sustained.

CONTEMPLATE: Intensity

ASK YOURSELF: Do I overreact?

TELL YOURSELF: I am in control of my emotions.

KNOW: Short-lived emotional intensity can have permanent consequences.

Notes:

MOTHER OF WATER
(QUEEN OF CUPS)

It is natural to keep some parts of ourselves hidden, but pent up emotions can be a destructive form of isolation.

CONTEMPLATE: Isolation

ASK YOURSELF: Do I fear sharing my emotions?

TELL YOURSELF: What I feel is important and should be expressed.

KNOW: Repressed emotions are harmful burdens that will eventually erupt.

Notes:

Father of Water
(King of Cups)

A simple act of lending a hand or reaching out to someone makes a big difference. Love is healing.

Contemplate: Healing

Ask Yourself: Am I willing to give support to others?

Tell Yourself: I am not afraid to get involved.

Know: An act of kindness from one to another, heals both.

Notes:

The Father of Water Experience

Begin your relaxation process and when you are comfortable, close your eyes. The first thing you become aware of is the sound of waves, splashing against the shoreline. You are at the edge of the sea. Light dances on the water. A long pier stretches out over the ocean and you feel compelled to walk upon it. Up ahead you hear the sound of a chattering dolphin. Further down the pier, you see a man sitting on the edge, his feet dangling in the water. You can also see the dolphin stretching up toward him, half way out of the water. The man is feeding the dolphin from a silver bucket at his side. As he reaches down, the dolphin rises up and nuzzles his hand. There is a feeling of love and nurturing connected to this scene. It moves over you and fills you. Sit down next to the Father of Water and become a part of this moment. Spend some time here talking to the Father, feeding the dolphin, and experiencing the healing energy that love creates. When you are ready, open your eyes and begin journaling your experiences.

Notes:

ONE OF AIR
(ACE OF SWORDS)

The mind has unlimited potential, both positive and negative. Clarity of perception separates truth from illusion.

CONTEMPLATE: Clarity

ASK YOURSELF: Do I control my thoughts or allow them to control me?

TELL YOURSELF: I begin to see clearly.

KNOW: Every negative thought can be replaced by a positive one.

Notes:

The One of Air Experience

Begin your relaxation process and when you are comfortable, close your eyes. You feel the sensation of a gentle breeze that blows against your face. The smell of salt is in the air. In the distance, waves crash against a coastline. There is white sand beneath your feet and the sun shines down from the blue sky above. All around you, growing from the sand are tall yellow sea oats, gently swaying in the breeze. It is a beautiful place. You spend a moment or two taking it all in. The gentle breeze becomes steadier, blowing against your skin and hair. It moves over you and seems to move through you. It is a cleansing breeze and this is your opportunity to release. Let go of unwanted thoughts, ideas and negative energy. Feel them leave your body and dissipate into the wind. Now allow the breeze to fill you with clarity, truth, and optimism. Spend a few moments here, gathering and releasing. When you are ready, open your eyes and begin journaling your experiences. You can return to the sea oats whenever you feel the need to cleanse or release.

Notes:

Two of Air
(Two of Swords)

Sometimes even when we know what needs to be done we hesitate, because we are unwilling to take responsibility for our choices.

Contemplate: Responsibility

Ask Yourself: Do I accept responsibility for my choices?

Tell Yourself: I make decisions without fear.

Know: There are no wrong choices.

Notes:

Three of Air
(Three of Swords)

Expectations are not wrong, but being too attached to a specific outcome leads to disappointment.

Contemplate: Expectation

Ask Yourself: Do my expectations limit me?

Tell Yourself: I am flexible.

Know: If something didn't happen the way it was expected, then it wasn't supposed to.

Notes:

FOUR OF AIR
(FOUR OF SWORDS)

Rest is essential. It is important to take time out to recharge and gather strength on all levels.

CONTEMPLATE: Rest

ASK YOURSELF: Do I nurture myself?

TELL YOURSELF: I allow myself to heal.

KNOW: Choosing to rest is a sign of wisdom, not weakness.

Notes:

FIVE OF AIR
(FIVE OF SWORDS)

Deception exists in the world. We are responsible for our own well-being and can only be deceived if we allow it.

CONTEMPLATE: Deception

ASK YOURSELF: How vulnerable am I to deceit?

TELL YOURSELF: I choose honesty.

KNOW: Dishonesty is a terrible waste of thought.

Notes:

Six of Air
(Six of Swords)

Life is a continuous journey with many twists and turns. Whatever is not working can be left behind and we can start over.

Contemplate: Journey

Ask Yourself: Is it time for a change?

Tell Yourself: I am ready to take the next step, wherever it leads.

Know: The Universe, including everything and everyone within it, is always moving.

Notes:

The Six of Air Experience

Sometimes it is necessary for us to just get away for a little while. If you are unable to escape physically, you always can in meditation. Begin your relaxation process and when you are comfortable, close your eyes. Imagine that you are driving down a country highway. You are the only car on the road. It is a pleasant day. On both sides of you there are beautiful views of green pastures dotted with tall trees. You are comfortable, relaxed, and enjoying the drive. There is no place you have to be and nothing you have to do. This is your opportunity to escape. You can choose any destination you desire or you can simply enjoy the ride. Take as much time as you need. Don't think about anything else. When you are ready open your eyes and journal your experiences. The car will be waiting for your next journey.

Notes:

Seven of Air
(Seven of Swords)

What we think, do, or say we draw to us. If we are honest, we will be treated with integrity. If we are dishonest, we will be taken advantage of.

Contemplate: Integrity

Ask Yourself: Am I ever dishonest?

Tell Yourself: I attract positive energy.

Know: Integrity is easier than dishonesty. It is more complicated and stressful to lie.

Notes:

EIGHT OF AIR
(EIGHT OF SWORDS)

Fear is a necessary reaction when danger is near. Unfounded, it becomes distorted into an overwhelming limitation.

CONTEMPLATE: Fear

ASK YOURSELF: Do I allow fear to control my life?

TELL YOURSELF: There is nothing to fear.

KNOW: Fear is a self-imposed prison.

Notes:

Nine of Air
(Nine of Swords)

Nothing has ever been solved by worrying. It closes the mind's ability to find solutions.

Contemplate: Worry

Ask Yourself: Do I create anxiety needlessly?

Tell Yourself: I focus on results, not problems.

Know: Worry serves no purpose but to cause additional stress.

Notes:

Ten of Air
(Ten of Swords)

No matter what happens to us, we will move beyond the current moment. At the end of every cycle, there is always renewal.

Contemplate: Renewal

Ask Yourself: Am I able to see beyond challenges?

Tell Yourself: I choose a positive outlook.

Know: A positive perspective creates new opportunities.

Notes:

CHILD OF AIR
(PAGE OF SWORDS)

Optimism is the excitement and wonder of an awakened mind, which embraces new ideas.

CONTEMPLATE: Optimism

ASK YOURSELF: Am I excited about future possibilities?

TELL YOURSELF: I allow my thoughts the freedom to grow.

KNOW: A mind, unhampered by doubts and fears, cultivates new ideas which can change the world.

Notes:

YOUTH OF AIR
(KNIGHT OF SWORDS)

An independent mind is not changed by the influence of others. Growth comes from within and through personal experience.

CONTEMPLATE: Independence

ASK YOURSELF: Am I free to be myself?

TELL YOURSELF: I can do anything I think I can.

KNOW: There is no conformity in a free mind.

Notes:

Mother of Air
(Queen of Swords)

Judgment is understanding the facts of a situation and making decisions based on that truth.

Contemplate: Judgment

Ask Yourself: Do I judge without knowing the facts?

Tell Yourself: I am open to the truth.

Know: Truth cannot be swayed by emotion.

Notes:

FATHER OF AIR
(KING OF SWORDS)

It takes a great deal of strength to be honest, especially with ourselves.

CONTEMPLATE: Honesty

ASK YOURSELF: Who am I?

TELL YOURSELF: I am truthful with myself.

KNOW: Honesty is the highest level of self-control.

Notes:

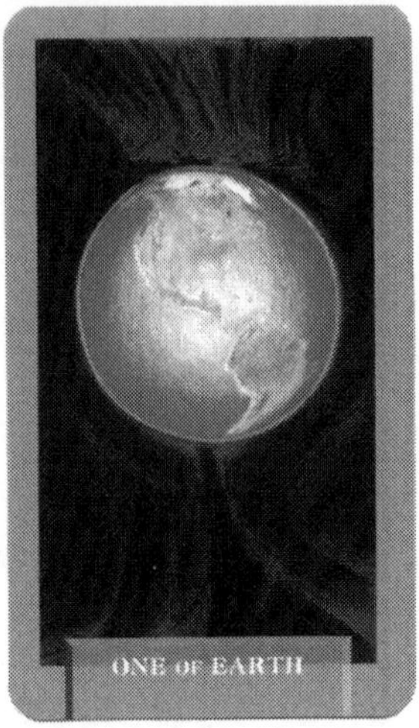

ONE OF EARTH
(ACE OF PENTACLES)

The Universe is abundant. There are no limits to our ability to grow.

CONTEMPLATE: Growth

ASK YOURSELF: How do I limit my growth?

TELL YOURSELF: I am constantly evolving.

KNOW: All growth is positive, even if it doesn't seem like it at the time.

Notes:

Two of Earth
(Two of Pentacles)

Priorities are necessary to achieve our goals. Each step should be accomplished according to its importance and what is unnecessary released.

Contemplate: Priorities

Ask Yourself: Have I lost sight of my goals?

Tell Yourself: I focus on one thing at a time.

Know: Divided attention accomplishes little.

Notes:

Three of Earth
(Three of Pentacles)

It is important for us to recognize our abilities and be proud of what we have accomplished. Creativity must be nurtured to grow.

Contemplate: Pride

Ask Yourself: Do I value what I have achieved?

Tell Yourself: I am proud of myself.

Know: Even the smallest contribution can make a great difference in the world.

Notes:

The Three of Earth Experience

Begin your relaxation process and when you are comfortable, close your eyes. You find yourself in the middle of a large art gallery. Lighted exhibits line the walls and displays of sculpture stand in the center of the room. As you walk forward you find room after room of art. There are displays of different styles from contemporary to abstract. One room contains the images of Tarot cards from Today's Journey Tarot. There is wonder, mysteries, and beauty all around. Begin to feel yourself drawn to a particular room. This room has a style of art that appeals to you. The images you see depicted, hold a message. It is as if the room itself is speaking. Its language is imagery, symbol, and metaphor. Spend some time in this room deciphering the clues given to you. They are significant at this time. Be open. When you are ready, open your eyes and begin journaling your experiences.

Notes:

FOUR OF EARTH
(FOUR OF PENTACLES)

We exist in a material world, but sometimes forget we are more than just physical. What is within truly sustains us.

CONTEMPLATE: Vanity

ASK YOURSELF: Do I see beyond outward appearances?

TELL YOURSELF: I look within to find my true self.

KNOW: Fulfillment does not come from vanity, the attainment of material things, or adornments.

Notes:

FIVE OF EARTH
(FIVE OF PENTACLES)

Our emotions can sometimes paralyze us. When we cannot see beyond the present situation, it is impossible to move forward.

CONTEMPLATE: Stagnation

ASK YOURSELF: What am I waiting for?

TELL YOURSELF: I can move forward.

KNOW: Staying in one place is a choice. Not moving is not living.

Notes:

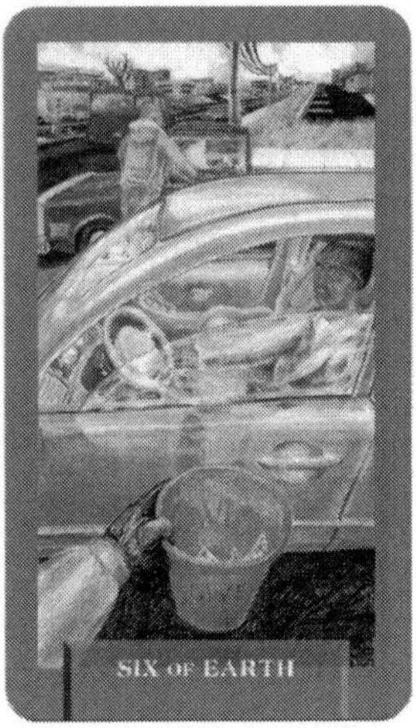

SIX OF EARTH
(SIX OF PENTACLES)

We must learn how to give in order to receive. Often we contribute without a charitable heart.

CONTEMPLATE: Charity

ASK YOURSELF: How do I give?

TELL YOURSELF: I have enough to share.

KNOW: True charity has no reservations, resentments, or expectations.

Notes:

SEVEN OF EARTH
(SEVEN OF PENTACLES)

Once we have done everything necessary for a desired outcome, there is nothing left to do. We must be patient.

CONTEMPLATE: Patience

ASK YOURSELF: Do I worry about what I can't control?

TELL YOURSELF: It is okay to just wait.

KNOW: Everything happens in its own time.

Notes:

Eight of Earth (Eight of Pentacles)

Talent is not limited to the arts or entertainment. We have the ability to master skills in any area.

Contemplate: Talent

Ask Yourself: What are my strengths?

Tell Yourself: I recognize my abilities.

Know: Talents are gifts from the Universe meant to be cultivated.

Notes:

NINE OF EARTH
(NINE OF PENTACLES)

We have abundance, even when it is not apparent. Everything we need and more, is available to us.

CONTEMPLATE: Abundance

ASK YOURSELF: Am I aware of my prosperity?

TELL YOURSELF: I have everything I need.

KNOW: There is a difference between want and need.

Notes:

Ten of Earth
(Ten of Pentacles)

Experience leaves its own legacy. The past is a teacher that should not be viewed as a burden or with regret.

Contemplate: Legacy

Ask Yourself: Does my past weigh me down?

Tell Yourself: I learn from my experiences.

Know: Every moment offers an opportunity to grow.

Notes:

Child of Earth
(Page of Pentacles)

Curiosity leads to new discoveries. Only by stretching our mind and enhancing our talent can we reach our potential.

Contemplate: Curiosity

Ask Yourself: Do I limit my possibilities?

Tell Yourself: I am willing to grow.

Know: The world is filled with magic and wonder, waiting to be discovered.

Notes:

YOUTH OF EARTH
(KNIGHT OF PENTACLES)

Stability gives us the confidence to reach higher. It is how we recharge and find balance.

CONTEMPLATE: Stability

ASK YOURSELF: Where do I find stability in my life?

TELL YOURSELF: I have a strong foundation.

KNOW: The strength of the roots determine the height of the tree.

Notes:

The Youth of Earth Experience

Begin your relaxation process and when you are comfortable, close your eyes. You find yourself, along with a small group of people, at the mouth of a large cave. A young man is speaking. He is a tour guide who will lead your group through the cave. A cool breeze escapes the entrance as you begin to work your way inside. Modern lighting and walkways have been installed to make walking easier. As you move further into the cave you are attracted to its features. There are massive, smooth walls all around and stalactites reach down from above. There is a sense of stability here and the endurance of the earth. You feel a connection to its strength. It is grounding. No matter what is going on above in your life, this place allows you to connect with the balance within. Like the earth itself, it give you support and strength. You absorb this earth energy. Spend some time exploring the cave with the group, guide, or on your own. Allow its energy to flow into you and remain with you even when you leave this place. When you are ready, open your eyes and begin journaling your experiences. The cave will be there whenever you feel the need for grounding, stability, or support.

Notes:

MOTHER OF EARTH
(QUEEN OF PENTACLES)

It is important to care for others, but nurturing ourselves is a vital aspect of unconditional love.

CONTEMPLATE: Nurturing

ASK YOURSELF: Do I love myself?

TELL YOURSELF: I treat myself with compassion.

KNOW: An open heart is all inclusive.

Notes:

Father of Earth
(King of Pentacles)

Everything we think, do, and say has an effect which endures. The purity of our intent determines whether that effect is positive or negative.

Contemplate: Endurance

Ask Yourself: Is what I create positive?

Tell Yourself: What I do matters.

Know: One ripple across a pond changes its surface forever.

Notes:

Conclusion

The Tarot never stops teaching. There is always more to learn. This book is a stepping stone to deeper levels of understanding of the Tarot and yourself.

Meditation never stops revealing. It illuminates who you really are and how you can elevate yourself to your highest potential.

Together they are the ultimate tool for self-awareness. As you continue with your meditation practices and study of the Tarot your link within grows stronger, opening you to new worlds of spiritual enlightenment, transformation, and discovery.

For more information contact www.todaysjourneytarot.com

About Expanding Dimensions

Expanding Dimensions, was formed in 2003, and is comprised of five members whose combined knowledge of the Tarot and meditation encompasses nearly a century of experience. They co-authored *Today's Journey Tarot* which was published in 2011 and *Today's Journey Tarot, A Traveler's Guide*, published in 2013. More information on Today's Journey Tarot can be found at todaysjourneytarot.com.

John Lavey began his interest in the esoteric during his extensive study of religion at a catholic school, Flaget High School located in Louisville, Kentucky. John continued the study of religion through his college years at Western Kentucky University. He began studying the Tarot twenty years ago and has read professionally. John lives in a small rural community near Louisville, Kentucky with his wife, daughter, and dog, Brodie. He enjoys long walks in the woods.

Pat Lavey co-authored Today's Journey Tarot with her spouse John and the other members of Expanding Dimensions. Over twenty years ago her interest in the Tarot began in order to understand psychic events which had occurred in her life. Pat has read and taught the Tarot enjoying the experience of giving others the help the Tarot offers. She graduated from Indiana University and has enjoyed diverse careers. Pat takes solace in her rural home in Indiana believing, "Nature always wears the colors of the spirit."-Emerson

Teresa Sue McAdams, Ph.D. earned a doctorate of Philosophy in Parapsychic Science. Sue is a full time teacher of Tarot, meditation, spiritual development and tai chi. It was in Sue's classes that the members of Expanding Dimensions met. She is the author of *Lessons: The Wisdom Within Each Moment*. Sue has worked professionally as a tarot reader since 1988, doing private readings, psychic fairs and events. She is married to co-author Ben Perry.

Ben Perry is the author of *Journeys: A Guide to Group Meditation*. He is the creator of benperrymeditations.com a resource website for his meditation CDs, downloads, books and more. It includes meditations for children, groups, behavior modification and new age. Ben has been reading Tarot and teaching and leading meditation since 1988 and has given lectures at area schools, churches, books stores and learning centers. Ben and Sue live across the river from Louisville, Kentucky with their three cats, Thai, Lily, and Melody.

Bonnie Taylor is a Reiki Master who has dedicated herself to the healing arts. Bonnie holds a B.S. degree in Architectural Drafting and History and has spent the last twenty years enhancing her knowledge of metaphysics. During the course of her study, Bonnie became interested in the Tarot and has participated in psychic fairs and events. Bonnie meditates regularly and is a 1st Degree Black Belt in Tae Kwon Do. She lives in Louisville with her dog, Mia.

TERESA SUE MCADAMS, BONNIE TAYLOR, BEN PERRY, JOHN LAVEY, PAT LAVEY

About the Illustrator

Christopher Wilkey is an illustrator, graphic designer, and muralist, who holds a B.F.A. in Studio Art and an A.A.S. in Computer Graphic Design, as well as having majored in Art at Louisville's duPont Manual Magnet High School. He has been pursuing drawing consciously since the age of seven. A student of Art History, he has found influence in wide ranging movements and artists throughout, but Pablo Picasso, Salvador Dali, M.C. Escher, Alberto Giacometti, and Alex Grey count among those by whom he is influenced. He first encountered information on the Tarot as a child in a book from his family's library that dealt with psychic and esoteric phenomena.

13464695R00109

Printed in Great Britain
by Amazon.co.uk, Ltd.,
Marston Gate.